metabolics

poems

metabolics

JESSICA E. JOHNSON

ACRE

CINCINNATI 2023

Acre Books is made possible by the support of the
Robert and Adele Schiff Foundation and the
Department of English at the University of Cincinnati.

ISBN-13 (pbk) 978-1-946724-57-1
ISBN-13 (ebook) 978-1-946724-58-8

Designed by Barbara Neely Bourgoyne
Cover art: *Cedar, Salal* by Marita Wai, cyanotype on watercolor paper,
8 in. x 12 in.

The press is based at the University of Cincinnati, Department of
English and Comparative Literature, Arts & Sciences Hall, Room 248,
PO Box 210069, Cincinnati, OH, 45221-0069.

Acre Books books may be purchased at a discount for educational use.
For information please email business@acre-books.com.

for
those who feel their strangeness

contents

metabolics

HEREIN

Biology is an enormous subject, one that can seem overwhelming to students and scientists alike. In the lecture hall I missed a lot. One rich diagram about cascades could unleash in me cascades of thought, cocoon me in imagining and boom the hour was up. I loved to *make connections* and *study the figures.* I did not learn what they wanted.

They wanted us to learn what companies can use. I wanted to transform the way I see.

Textbook pages told cycles, cycles within cycles: the efficient workings of the living. I desired ferns and fur and skin. I loved the living, so why not the machine of them? I loved the drawings of metabolic pathways where excess product blunts production. The language of balance, arrows feeding compounds back into the reaction. Elegant self-regulation. The new created, not too much.

—

A long time later I came to live in a house on the edge of a forest, sleeping under cedars every night, my offspring in the next room growing furiously with sleep. Cedar is *Thuja plicata,* western red. *All cedars have scaly, fern-like needles that tend to overlap.* They do not point or pierce. Cedar fills my window, a great green lacing down—countless fingers, new tips of bright growth.

She anchors the system, sharing air with fir and maple above the groundling sword fern and mahonia and snowberry. She needs a lot of space to make the shade. Her seedlings spindle up everywhere. Few grow into giants but when they do, they stay.

Cedar offers *birds and wildlife year-round cover from predators and bad weather, along with places to roost, rest and nest.* Butterflies embed their ova in her bark. Gray squirrels scamper-cling along her giant trunk, their bodies splayed to barely hold her. When I say *cedar*, I mean mother. When I say *cedar*, I mean being the main thing.

—

At home in the house on the edge of the forest, at work for the college on the outskirts of the city, tending two children, two animals, and countless plants, balancing energetic expenditure always with a spouse, responsible for the learning of hundreds of students every year, I'm pulled in circles and pushed by arrows, each day carrying out cycles, each day-cycle subsumed in sets of larger cycles. Job and sweat and screen time and so many kinds of holding. Daily reprieve, generational harm. All of us lodged in words that end with -ism like shell bits tumbling in a tide. Birth and the death inside of it, joy and the panic it can spark. The troublesome design I call myself: worn down and regenerating, locked in exchange and conversion, trading in the currencies of energy.

Some pathways result in more instead of less: *positive* feedback, where the product turns its own production up. Platelets clotting a wound release compounds that draw more platelets in. The textbook example is childbirth, hormones contracting the womb in ever-amplifying waves until one body exits another. Let me be clear: the body I sometimes wish to exit is my own.

—

Herein I translate my own *here* into small reactions whose products float as if inside a giant body—atmospheric, accreting.

The larger situation proliferates a culture: well-intentioned harm; indifference with eyes trained on acquisition. What follows might be read as a long attention to microscopic, daily countervailing forces.

What follows might be read as one poem turning through reactions of stasis and conversion.

What follows might be read as a woman up in the dark burning a candle, spilling words in the rationed minutes when no one needs her—until the sky lightens.

What follows might be read as a domestic sphere wishing to declare itself a microcosm.

What follows wishes to be considered an organism in the balance of self-maintenance and change.

What follows is another walking sac of carbon in a climate made too warm by too much carbon, the sac of carbon never not-thinking about its own excess.

Atmospheric, accreting: what follows sometimes forms a cloudland. Heavy air takes on more weight and then it rains.

OF DAYLIGHT SAVING TIME, MYFITNESSPAL, AND INDOOR/OUTDOOR CATS

Fig.

Body of trees a block of dark outside the home-office
your body your attention pending here before the
day's reactions and—

       the way dark cedars suck light from
sky the way dark hills suck light from air the trees
       more perfect black more perfect black
       until the flood of daylight.

//

Daylight equals lists and tasks. Each item on the tasklist signifies a body in a place doing something it has come to consider important *buy plants dentist grading kids room workout* each task containing an array of other tasks the regular life proliferating its own maintenance its packaging inevitably forming the substrate of the day-plan the detritus attracting itself, coalescing.

Day's abrasions produce excess feeling. Someone okay several someones did not reply. Most everyone forgot to mention. The *colleague* asserted his in fact pretty limited expertise by telling you how things *actually* are the screen's particular kind of light swelling a bit of brain restricting blood to the ocular until the world chafes vision and the wind the trees the clouds feel built for harm.

In efforts to avoid an untimely release of Excess Feeling in efforts to make your body less you commence workout which eats with its molecular teeth pooled up Excess Feeling. The device records your motion translates you into an equation. You respire heavily on campus sweating your foundation wearing clothes not meant for anyone to see.

//

Home: before the day starts birds eat away at silence.
Their twitter nibbles darkness into lace the printer hums
because you didn't think to turn it off.

The devices eat electrons and electrons and electrons
which come from a spilled river which come from a coal
fire and the river spills salmon bodies and the coal fire
blooms heat and the devices yield heat and the cherry
trees swell early and the summer kills. Outlets wait for
the prongs of devices.

Cat wears her only clothes. Touch cat and she chirps.
(Touch—chirp. Touch—chirp.)

The regular life eats money the cars eat money each
device needs its own cover each life in your home in fact
needs coverage and money eats time and even before the
day starts well before the dark sky erupts in birdsong—

Cat the beloved specimen the invasive species cat the little piece of midnight velvet attaches briefly to carpet storing up energy her characteristic throat music the sound that first endeared you to her that persuaded you to choose her to feed and warm and watch over her furred body with its bits of sharp despite. Cat too: charging.

//

Despite so many attempts to resolve this tension, sometimes you are *you* and also sometimes *mother* just as light can be both particle and wave a person sometimes other times a role and no one can locate you at any particular time on that continuum of *you* and *mother* at best the observers (you the self-observer) could assign a probability.

Mother's precursor is *girl* or at least that's what they called you a half-naked self-decorating body dirt-smeared making songs from anything. Girl, a kind of song-being.

Mother was a girl who never saw a long-needled pine a street-side locust a groomed red maple without wanting to inhabit it wanting to wave just like it wanting to glow just like it wanting a shape just like it.

(And what shapes can you inhabit now? When the cat
the children keep homing to your body when they take
some special kind of respite in your warmth. You inhale
the boy's fresh hairline brush your lips against the girl's
right ear.)

//

The cedar's lower story fills the home-office window. In mental reactions cedar catalyzes language: *auntie, ruffled, feathers*. Wind combs the white sky.

Wind plus cedars equals the motion of ghosts outside the bedroom window the sway putting the children to sleep. The children dreamed in utero or so you've read, blind bulbs startling in response to images they could only have inherited.

And you. Cedar's dancing finger-fronds take up your ambition in the night and you wake as an inert gas not reacting to children or the *ping ing ing ing* devices.

Imagine you and the cedar arrange a psychic trade: you as she and she as you. She wakes at one resting her head on the dark sky pillow. You shed your inner soldier and feel the spread of your roots, your rising fluids. The cedar turns over a stupid thing she said at work remembers moments when she may have offended someone. You may live to be one thousand years old dry spells and fire notwithstanding. Cedar considers all the ways in which she's not enough, how her hundred feet aren't tall enough to make a home. Cedar tries coming up with ways of being better, being someone else, being something else and you—close your leaf pores to the cooler air, host a grand reaction, your body restoring itself from stored up light.

Morning, pores close, the exchange over. Run hands along your thick red bark. Flood of daylight produces the cat, coming in from murder.

//

OF METABOLISM

You convert fat into breath the legs metabolizing. You go to elaborate lengths to help the body exchange mass for air, consume more of itself. You eat only. You do not eat until. You run faster you fast you run *fasted*. For weeks you enter every food consumed into the device. You enter every food consumed into the device. You enter every food consumed and the device rewards you with digital confetti and balloons. You a shape that could be different you a mind that could enforce a change in shape you a face you cannot see lit by the sudden screenglow.

The boy and girl eat very little they burn the strange fuel
their bodies were born with. The boy and girl lick crystals
white or brown refined or raw juiced from a cane sold
cheap everywhere to shape children's palates. Mixed just
a little into everything. The child eyes wild, the children
build and build. Asleep their cheeks look sculpted out
of gorgeous fat.

The dog eats hours converts whole days into whimper
and sleek eats space later in fetch mode looping one ball
back to one spot spitting it out and spitting it out the dog
bred to carry dead birds back to the gunman but now—

And now you have no gun no ammo. The dog cannot retrieve a bird. Twice a day you feed her meat-scented pellets made of who-knows-what to catalyze her whimpered dreamsong her feet twitching after animals she's never seen but smelled.

Investigation loops back to one spot. You're entangled in artifacts of history: at play at work asleep in bad bones. You your body in this place an artifact of history the whiskered creatures pacing your house.

//

Sky eats space touching down on all slash each of us. Sky consumes smoke and holds it—holds it—before its great devastating exhalations. Sky takes on dimension like an inverted pool. You only understand when a plane cuts through one hot day on the lakeshore with friends and all slash each of you feeding on slash producing jokes until the jokes accrue in an indefinite mass that inhibits further jokes and forms a pool of warm silence.

The boy and girl produce marks on paper they carry the papers in across the threshold and they spill. Secretly the recycling bin swallows them while the children engage in other reactions and you retreat to a darkened room writing letters of atonement to the forest. The forest: a stable slow structure that doesn't speak an alphabetic language. The forest produces debris and ash it is thought to have myriad functions not all of them well understood.

The rain eats ambition and produces a green glaze on steps and railings and the hood of the car. The moss's substrate is mineral: old rock washed gently away from itself. No inhibition: when there's too much moss there's just more moss.

Flame consumes paraffin and throws off shadows. The boy and girl throw off accomplishments and eat more crystals.

//

The longer day provokes a general swelling cats pushing through cracked doorways at dawn. We show more skin. Brain produces early-wake. Texts fly between nodes of geographically dispersed friend networks. The mechanism by which texts fly is poorly understood.

Last night, in the city unexpectedly, dropping something for a friend: You could have eaten it the warm air the darkening streets the blossoms erupted like fanfare. You couldn't eat it. You drifted with wet hair swum limbs past the collection of bare armed people chewing through smoke and amber liquids. You would have reacted thus some time ago taken in the night in packs and rounds and woken up knowing the hours had done something to you.

//

The forest eats what it can of the city's monstrous growing heat. The treemass respires through microscopic leaf-pores inhaling the car's breath inhaling the house's breath building its own body of carbon gathering sunlight in the canopy while we walk the cool-field below.

Later in the home office your hands convert nerve-
impulses into keystrokes. Heart powers blue blood
into red blood into blue again. Blood blushes the lungs
the lungs mirroring the branching forms outside the
window the trees upright and breathing the forest and
your insides breathing in parallel pink and green pink
and green and thoracic and canopy and—

//

1. Before the Children Were Born

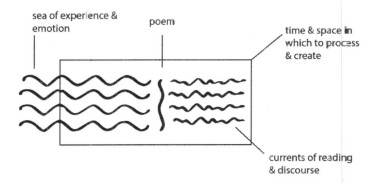

sea of experience & emotion

poem

time & space in which to process & create

currents of reading & discourse

2. After

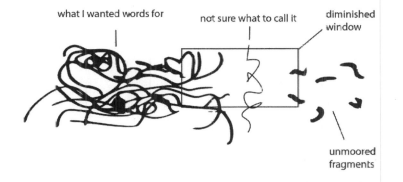

what I wanted words for

not sure what to call it

diminished window

unmoored fragments

Figure: Two Writing Lives

Key Terms

adjective: plastic

1.

made of plastic

not genuine; artificial or unnatural

2.

(of a substance or material) easily shaped or molded.

exhibiting adaptability to change or variety in the environment.

offering scope for creativity.

OF CLOUDLAND, OF PLASTICLAND

Fig.

Two things about here: heavy cloud
covers us two hundred and twenty-two days a year.
On graphs the population line rises skyward.

Fig.

Fog consumes the treetops, takes
them swimming in itself. A cloud-lake
touches down.

//

Here in beautiful sought-after Cloudland the city is a
known utopia of street trees an invisible map of circular
havens a spectacular *keeping out of.* A series of *awkward
moments.* The city eats the sensation of belonging and
sells it back in the form of hand-crafted in the form of
kombucha in the form of zoning in the form of programs
in the form of bike paths in the form of curated produce.

The boy the girl produce war games sword play and songs against each other's bodies. Each wants the most of what there is. Each carries a blanket ready to cover the other's hurt. Each ready to wrap the other in arms. They break the forest and cradle its debris.

The boy and girl find *mother* ask for *mother* find her cheek
her neck: all this *together* pools. The cat the dog arrive
sensing *together* find *mother* taken up. The cat, the dog
adhere to one another, watching.

In day the heat of grown bodies. In night the flood of home. In a pool of much, the arms aren't sufficient, the—

//

Cloudland fails to curate its plastic. Pages eat ink and pens used up leave plastic husks. Nothing digests plastic. Activity throws off small acts of plastic. Our clothing sheds filaments of plastic. Seabirds take up plastic. Whales take up plastic. People try quitting plastic for one month and say it's very hard. We all take up plastic and live.

The children told the trees about their favorite shows: *My Little Pony Magic School Bus Barbie Secret Agents.* The trees said nothing so the children screamed their songs. You lay at the base of one tree watching leaves sky their way down to the floor. Even here you open in your mental browser tab after tab your feelings ill-defined and looking for a site to touch down.

You unfold and touch down on children who have plentiful receptors and produce strange verbal constructions with no apparent use except the delight of mother except this flood of cheeks and arms.

//

The same ones again: waking up in a rotting house, trying to stop a car with bad brakes. Dreams unzip and replicate themselves piece by piece.

//

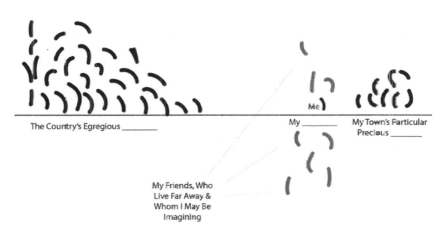

The Country's Egregious _____

Me

My _____

My Town's Particular
Precious _____

My Friends, Who
Live Far Away &
Whom I May Be
Imagining

Figure: I Have Lived in Cloudland for Fifteen Years

OF SMALL DEVICES

We used to place the telephones in cradles but now
they are no longer baby-like no they are thin portals to
vast streams the way in dreams a small thing unlocks
something very large.

We wake to our feeds in a house with a little land around it next to other houses with a little land around them more land than anyone needs and less land than people need in common and to maintain this house to fold lovingly each of its garments to trim its edges shape its shapable shrubs could be a person's full-time job. Your energy now taken up by your feed by the emotional exoskeleton of text threads with their fibrous connection to all your feelings all your cherished bullshit. You take *a break* you open tabs consuming abstract notions of students' ideal functioning and children's ideal functioning and the body's ideal functioning.

The students gather in classrooms and silence their feeds. The reaction called learning is often thought to be inefficient learning is a constellation of individual reactions in which the *instructor* competes in the student's mind with formations originating elsewhere and no one is sure if learning has in fact taken place.

It is in fact your job to measure learning the products of which are unclear.

The students' feeds their threads pile information silently the students have stored in their mind whatever feeds their imaginations whatever makes them feel okay for this hour. You are standing in front of them *checking in* on their learning you feel your own feed humming in the pocket.

After the children are in bed you check the feed the feed unlocks the compound known as rage a belligerent famous face catalyzes in a cage around the heart the antique lace of impotence and danger. The strange round hole of the man's mouth. Even all stirred up he cares to hide his crooked childhood teeth now super white and straight. You recognize that your hatred is feeding him somehow he consumes it and he swells.

The formations of the feed, the text thread webs proliferate unchecked. The forest you live beside was meant to burn. The groundling species tinder first and maples burn the cedar though built to char and still withstand. Wildfire now suppressed the overstory grows too thick the understory tinder-quick to catch.

//

OF WINTER GARDENS, CONFECTIONS,
AND ROUTINE HOLIDAY STRESS

Fig.

Lamp casts ghost shapes on the wall. Snowberry
(*Symphoricarpos hesperius*) goes cold, loses leaves,
appears as sticks dripping white globes. She decorates
herself by being less.

                                                    / /

The children are in love with whatever they can gather right now leaves right now cheap bracelets made of plastic right now stones right now. Leaves. They notice each and fill their pockets with about-to-decomp and mother she imagines lying down and papering herself with yellow dying shapes being nude and cold and covered so that that only her face would be visible.

Early night yields mindseye and winterbird and twig and flashback to deeper snows to sliding on blue ice sheet. To VCRs and take 'n' bake pizza to crust of exhaust on the snowbank and a prickling white sky promising wonderland sky wonderlanding down onto the visible earth when the weather was different.

Daily, the car consumes refined bones produces sicker sky. Stores crumbs, hair, spill. Car is the substrate of commute commute is a dry reaction eating minutes throwing off periodic sprays of dread.

In winter the city is a structure composed of reservoirs. Uber sails you past shop window reservoirs of fine consumer goods lit up in early-night. Reservoirs of fine decor, menu after menu. Reservoirs of shelter adjacent to reservoirs of blackberry to reservoirs of tents. Cyclists counter reservoirs with opposing force they stream across the city they expend.

The body keeps failing to be less. Confections in the shape of carved squash in the shape of ghosts follow the body to work after the night of children's masking. This luxury substance there's simply too much of too much resulting in an undesirable excess of body a pool of flesh you are capable of loving only when it's less.

//

On a predetermined date the family gathers in the living space for ritual exchange. In the season of snowberry mother's reactions are taken up entirely with consumer goods confections and the trimming of paper into shapes of snow the sky does not make here.

Driving away from ritual exchange, the fog and trees the light and trees line the freeway, form the story for you to speed through and the sometimes blue of trees the often black of trees the body of the forest-patch contains specimens live specimens dead species and bones. Birds and the bodies of birds and the soil made by cataclysmic comprehensible movements of the earth and moss and fallen limbs and blown debris. Seedlings sleep through the driest recorded winter.

//

People made the freeway made you a person driving now past Panera Bread past Mattress World Cabela's Rodda KFC Shari's on a sunken commuter lane that smells like fries. These structures these synthetics made to glow for twenty-four hours made not to sleep made to look as if they aren't right now gently losing value, softly breaking down.

Too many things again in the house. Imagine you create the first big box store made to decay everything in it built with a reasonable life-span before a predetermined return to nutrients. You call it Decomp R Us. The children's toys will one by one emit whiffs of rot and you and the children will carry them to the cedar's broad feet just as slime is forming on a stuffed animal's fur and the children will transfer their attachment from toys to cedar throwing their bodies against her tough and tender bark the ferns at her feet will extra-flourish.

//

At a slow rate you depreciate clothes cars microwaves printers phones chairs virgin teeth unwieldy items built to amuse children. The cat, the dog. Each item in your care however small however tangential carries a charge you perceive as the weight of its presence an energetic tax that pools in the synapses inhibiting your transformation and growth.

The boy, the girl watch *Baking Show* and conjure elaboration elaborating the simple with any available material taping bits of paper onto paper, paper made of failing forest clear magic tape made of question mark and unspooled from another piece of plastic.

Mother and father leave *Baking Show* and pick up their devices where they watch *Chef's Table* an episode specifically in which a nun touches every mushroom carefully. Mother and father dream of hours and simplicity they vow to get rid of everything they buy a book on fermentation and forget it's there.

//

The girl sheds teeth and gathers coins. Raspberry leaves yellow in the cold. The girl appears in the kitchen frozen toed with a cup full of broken berries and we all continue loving them though they're bruised the way the boy the girl father continue touching down on mother's body though it's begun to droop grown pale and soft and creased.

In bed he continues desiring your soft creased body from the device you consume tips on making your body look different. You conjure the body that looked a certain way back then he desired you same as now you ran miles in attempts to look like someone else.

The device prompts you when it's *Bedtime* and wakes you with recorded birdsong from a different season in another forest.

//

The Belly, Your Belly	Is Unclassifiable So	Read This Across
• I'm saying your belly	• Can't be a type any	• More than your elbow
• Can be a type.	• Like an elbow, your belly	• Is morally neutral, a sign of
• Nothing in particular. Like an	• Elbow, your belly might be	• Beautiful or ugly depending
• On who's in the room	• On the light and shadow and	• Circumstances.
• Covered or out, the belly	• Exists because your	• Mother's mother's mother
• Survived some shit.	• Imagine the chain of bellies	• Building, saving, hanging on
• To themselves through bad	• Harvests, war, scarce game	• So that you could be born.
• A Belly has carried you in the	• Beginning, or in the most	• Recent little ending. The belly
• Cannot be traded, bought, or	• Meaningfully processed. It's	• Molecular. It's you. It's yours.

Figure: They Try to Sell You a Thing According to "Belly Type"

OF KNOWLEDGE:
THE VAST, PROVISIONAL BODY

On a weekend in full daylight you crave the compounds released by decomp you rest your padded bones on damp ground, on so many fragments of cedar, while the boy, the girl embark on *challenges*, climbing hills and fallen logs, teaching their bodies the shape of mountains.

The feed proclaims: *A Single Session of Exercise Alters 9,815 Molecules in Our Blood.* The pathways turn and we unlock ourselves.

Your eyes adjust and stars come out even in this Cloudland, this Plasticland, this place of fluxing hegemonies. You receive information not like posts in a feed but like compounds washed up against delicate root-hairs after rain, like CO_2 wafting into an open leaf pore.

Say one night after they're in bed the fridge humming you open up the screen door and step out. You full of night, night full of you. You listen to ferns whose roots store water you listen to salal whose leaves lose little water whose body paints the shape of flame whose berries hang right here. The *super/blood/wolf* moon now risen. Like the moon you have stopped counting what you feed yourself, the slice of apple in your mouth and gone before you realized you were holding the knife.

Elsewhere a whale falls feeding the seafloor. The backyard
was a seafloor once when the coastline was different and
may be so again the backyard holds your children now
your giggling earth-babies falling and rising and rising on
a trampoline in daylight.

What's conserved over so much time: the chemical
conspiracy between trees, between you and children,
entities in need with each other, bodies listening to
bodies.

//

Body feels the day coursing through it needs movement to consume pools of worry. Body walks itself into feeling different. Body decorates itself, paints its awnings, hangs rings on its unimportant skin. Body rests itself, tumbles into its sleep-time projection room. Body grown inside another body. Body surviving on the bones of other bodies. Body living because other bodies are consumable. Body into its own bullshit all day. Body doing what it did the day before. Body with cat. Body with children. Body taking up cosmetic attention, body inhaling the product of burnt plants, body inhaling the product of respiring plants. Body in motion, metabolizing rage. Whose body. Whose body. Having to say *I*.

//

Another day: the girl unfolds and touches down on you
unzipping the day reacting to stories of social positioning
of grade school power plays and small humiliations and
you let advice pool up unspoken do your best to cedar
that is to inhabit space and be the main home thing
without wanting to be less.

The girl and boy go forth into the yard look up at power lines and try crow-language opening their throats.

In the car the girl asks if you are *small* or *unsmall* and you say *yes*.

HEREIN

We gathered up damp bags and jackets, left the lecture hall, eventually for good. We fell out of campus and into the heavier gears of rent and hustle. We started building lists of small accomplishments. How to present ourselves as people *companies can use*? What kind of person is that? *What companies can use* is not a person.

Job to gig to sublet to lease to parking spot to parking ticket to bus to lunch break to hot plate to sleeplessness to sleep, we carried our dailiness. We tucked our dailiness in purses and messenger bags and touched it when we had a few minutes alone. We swam in our dailiness when drunk and woke up blank. Each turn through the day cycle formed part of a scheme, which is to say a story, which is to say an accidental self, too close to understand.

—

The few of us who teach don't do it like they did: not standing up in front of hundreds dealing info from the slide deck, not drawing out the long spool of predetermined facts and patterns for recall. If we have students, we tell them knowledge is something they build and rebuild.

And still without a test to pass systems and their ghostly representations have come at us, situating, telling us who we are.

In the days of widespread unemployment, graphs greeted us comparing this unemployment to the unemployment of generations past to the unemployment of other nations; the unemployment of our demographic groups; the days of widespread unemployment to the future date when more employment might arrive.

Who we are & also *what* & *how*. Pregnant the first time, was I comforted by peach-pink diagrams of what would happen? There was a lot they didn't show. The way she pressed into my lungs. My skin: smelling like a stranger's.

—

Genes, the consequential pieces of long molecule, sleep in an ingenious coil, nestled into vast repeats. Repeats: segments of seeming-nothing that may or may not matter.

The girl came and nudged awake the girl in me. She brought back every pop song I knew, viral fragments of tune, Stevie Wonder from the long-gone radio. *Isn't she lovely,* I whispered, afraid of being off-key as if my daughter was a spell that I could break.

When she was born, we lived in a different house, small, old with tall windows and loud neighbors all around. We lived on a wedge of land between two rivers. The soil was sand but it grew roses well.

She came and my perception telescoped *therein*: the house, her expressions and splayed fingers. I swelled. Her father swelled. We were all that kept her living. We no longer had a story of our own. We all survived and stopped appearing in public.

Therein milk flowed from my strange chest. My *chest* I would have called it then because men have them too; because a *chest* is also furniture; because it's a word you could say in company—not *tits* whispered in an ear, not *breasts,* a textbook word, one I'd long encountered only next to *cancer.*

It was summer and the house grew hot. Therein the baby rested on my thorax, the baby who didn't give a fuck, drank passionately, fought sleep passionately, slumbered passionately, who knew she would be heard and held, believed my body an extension of her own desires, believed that the universe extended out from her and so it did. When she napped, I thought of every danger past the door, in our time and before, the complex of them roused from history by her presence. *I thought* says the language of personal narration—although the thoughts just came. My daughter woke up an ancestral fear. I had no one to tell it to. Imagining was all that you could do.

—

Accounts of the body circulate. We take them in and they are incomplete. In which accounting can we understand love, and being loved, and all the ways that we might break?

One day at the table, the girl was drawing. "Is this really the shape of a heart?" she asked. We unlocked the device to watch the freakish beat. I drew the chambers, labeled the parts. She colored the empty blood, the full.

—

Herein this house I *self* sometimes like a beast. I sleep and sleep. Since I grew and expelled the children and the red placental interface—a ruffled blood-dense organ, grown and then discarded—I can't keep track of details. I read and eat as if I'm feeding something else.

Herein to hold my dailiness I have borrowed the language of certainty, played with assurance though there's no such thing.

Fact: the city's very bedrock travels clockwise at a speed imperceptible to the single human life, round some point south and east of here, round nowhere with a name. Motions out-span us.

Sometimes the center isn't you.

Or *you* are something more than you imagined.

notes

"Herein":

Italicized passages on western redcedar come from the "Cedar Identification" page on the Sciencing website and the "Ten Favorite Trees for Wildlife" page on the National Wildlife Federation blog.

Italicized passages on biology come from *Campbell Biology*, ninth edition (Reece, Urry, Cain, Wasserman, Winickoff, and Jackson, published by Benjamin Cummings, 2011).

"Of Knowledge: The Vast, Provisional Body":

The italicized headline in "The feed proclaims" comes from a *New York Times* article by Gretchen Reynolds, first published on June 10, 2020.

acknowledgments

This book is the lucky offspring of many parents. It grew from thick webs of support, companionship, and play, and it would not exist without the work of many.

Huge thanks to Lisa Ampleman, Nicola Mason, and Barbara Bourgoyne, all at Acre Books, and to Cassie Mannes Murray at Pine State Publicity.

Deep thanks to Marita Wai for the gorgeous cover art and the moving collaboration behind it.

Thanks to the following editors for publishing excerpts from this book: Olivia Cronk for publishing a version of "Of Winter Gardens, Confections, and Routine Holiday Stress" in Burning House Press's themed month of Studies in the (High) Gaudy Domestic on their site; Ander Monson for publishing "Of Daylight Saving Time, MyFitnessPal, and Indoor/Outdoor Cats" in *Diagram*; and Andrew S. Nicholson for publishing "Herein" and "Of Small Devices" for *Interim*; Isobel O'Hare and Carleen Tibbetts for publishing "Two Writing Lives," "I Have Lived in Cloudland for Fifteen Years," and "They Try to Sell You a Thing According to Belly Type" in *Dream Pop Journal*.

I'm especially grateful to Sara Wainscott for readings and relentless poetic companionship, and to Meredith Kimi Lewis for being the first to say *Keep working on this.*

I'm especially grateful to Camille T. Dungy and my Tin House workshop: Chenel King, Dāshaun Washington, Destiny Hemphill, Preeti Parikh, and Sarah Weck.

I'm grateful to Philip Sorenson: a line from his collection *Solar Trauma* sparked the first poem of this book. I'm grateful to Olivia Cronk, my brilliant friend-muse.

I'm grateful to Megan Snyder-Camp, Sonia Greenfield, Blake Hausman, Nicholas Hengen Fox, Jenine Fisher Harris, and Joon-Ae Haworth-Kaufka for friendship and encouragment.

I'm grateful to Laura Sanders and Sarah Tillery of Portland Community College for supporting my application for professional leave, and to the PCC Federation of Faculty and Academic Professionals for negotiating a contract that includes professional leave.

I'm especially grateful to Nadia Wallace and Jessica Amo for facilitating and making space for the writing group in which these poems first took root.

I'm grateful to my students in poetry, nonfiction, composition, and environmental literature, for being my thought partners as the book developed.

Thank you, Ingrid and Anders, for understanding that writing poems is a lot like playing Minecraft and that I need time and space to do it. May you surpass me in every way.

Thank you, George and Leslie Johnson, for your fundamental support.

Thank you, Kevin Edwards, for all the life you've brought me.